All You Need is *Love* (Notes)

Sweet Everythings For All the Loves in Your Life

By John Tabis

THE Bouqs CO.

UNIVERSE

I'd like to dedicate this journey to my parents,
Rae & Jooge, who through example taught me
just what true love is.

To my wife, **Kelly**: there are not close to enough blooms
in the world to express my love for you, but I'll keep
sending them anyway.

And finally to the **Bouqs fam**—our team,
farmers, and customers: thank you for making the
world a more beautiful place, one Bouq at a time.

—John

Introduction

Flowers are a gesture of kindness inspired by an array of emotions and moments. The simple act of gifting fresh blooms can spark a smile, rekindle an old connection, or bring laughter to the calamity of life. When receiving flowers, one instantly reaches for the note tucked gently among the petals. Who is it from? What does it say? This anticipation is invariably met with joy.

Each of those little messages, whether accompanying a bundle of hydrangeas or a triumphant mix of ranunculus, tells an intimate, private story.

All You Need Is Love (Notes) taps into sincere human interactions—between lovers, pals, family, or even pets. It can be a playful or encouraging note to self or a peek into a struggling poet searching for a word that rhymes with "roses are multicolored." (Spoiler alert: that word doesn't exist.)

Human beings naturally crave an authentic look into life's most honest moments, and this collection of real notes from real people offers a glimpse into the fascinating stories behind actual flower-delivery customers and their loved ones that represent the comedies and gravities of everyday life.

After a trying couple of years, the unwavering sentiment of flowers has not waned—nor have the millions of missives submitted with each The Bouqs Company order. In fact, I have witnessed the act of sending flowers blossom as a staple of social-distance connection. They became hugs disguised as bouquets, at a time when we all needed one.

Like Shakespearean sonnets among peonies, I hope this collection will be a gift to celebrate and savor, much like the blooms themselves.

John Tabis, FOUNDER & CHAIRMAN, THE BOUQS CO.

Gina,

The most beautiful part of these flowers is the person receiving them. I love you.

Brian

FAMILY

You are a strong, amazing father, stepfather, and father figure to your children, my children, and many young people in the world. Thank you for everything you do!

Dearest Tina,

I picked this bouquet just for you because it is aptly named "Paris," also known as "La Ville-Lumière" or "The City of Light." And you are the light that illuminates my world.

Love,
Charles

SWEET NOTHINGS

Fleurs? For moi? From who? Oh, yes, of course,
my adoring husband, who loves me best.

To the best doggie mom in the world!

Corona had the best life surrounded by those who loved him so much. Corona had brought everyone so much joy and happiness to everyone he met. May he rest in peace and enjoy all of the doggie bones in heaven!

We are here if you need anything at all!

Love you so much!
Tania, Kim, Jennie, Kayleigh, Ali & Ebby

LOVE

You are a wonderful and caring person, mom, and wife. I love you for just being you!

ANNIVERSARY LOVE

Happy anniversary, my love. I remember just yesterday when we first met. I hope we always keep it spontaneous and sexy. I love you until the end of time.

Love,
Kerline

TE AMO

I never anticipated to fall so hard for you, and now that I am here I cannot imagine life any other way. Te amo, when you're grumpy, when you're sleepy, when you're sad, when you're hungry, and especially when you're mad lol.

Te amo mucho mucho and I am so happy to be a part of the new journeys in your life.

Baby Julian, welcome to the world, my sweet! You are so loved already, more than I could ever express. Your parents are the best people, the best friends and will be the best parents— you are so lucky to have them! I can't wait to meet you in person.

All my love,
Rae

THANKFUL

This year, I'm most thankful for Andy's pouty face.

I guess maybe you too.

THINKING OF YOU

Because a good bouquet lasts longer than boys do. So proud of you and all you have accomplished!! You go, girl!!! Hint: These flowers look best beside a tray of brownies. Happy Valentine's Day!

You're just my favorite. That's all.

ROMANCE

Being in love is a lost art. The special moments lying in bed, laughing purely and with love. The gentle caress of a finger or a knowing nod. This is how I love you.

A strong person loves fiercely and FEELS. She allows tears as abundantly as laughter. He is both powerful but also tender, and can be spiritual and practical. A strong person is in essence a gift to the world.

We heard you were having a difficult time right now. While we know you'll get through this, we wanted to send you a little love because it's OK not to be OK. We're so lucky to have you as a cousin. We can't wait to see you in September. Until then, just know we love you no matter what. Just keep being you, because you're wonderful. Nothing can stop us. Let alone a little distance. Love you.

My Dearest: This particular bouquet is called "Dawn". With dawn comes the sun and you are the sun that came into my life almost two years ago during one of my darkest hours. Dawn also brings the promise of a new day and since we are in the dawn of our relationship, may the sun continue to rise and our love not be eclipsed. I love you.

Your One and Only,
Charles

I sat down today to copy down all the reasons
I love you. It took hours and I ran out of
paper. You are my perfect match—positive,
smart, fun-loving, mesmerizing, a complete
knockout and the best wife and mother. I will
work till the end of my days to make you smile.

Hubby

LOVE

To the woman who has it all. All my love, all my affection, and all my heart. All my trust, all my attention, and all my desire.

To the woman that has the most. The most wit, the most humor, the most class. The most beauty, the most kindness, the most sass.

To the woman who I will never stop. Never stop loving, never stop caring for, and never stop giving all that I am to.

FOR MY LADIES

These are for my ladies???!! I'm not always good at sending things on time for any particular occasion so this one is just because I love you ladies so much.

Love,
Sesa

SWEET NOTHINGS

I want to dance with you in the moonlight,
woodland bright among the sparkling fireflies.
These flowers are fairies, and you are my Queen.

Take a "deep breath" and remember you're not alone when missing Gamma. I miss her every day, tears are there, just not as often. Smile when thinking of her—she would want that.

If nothing else, maybe you'll find comfort
in knowing you are stuck with me forever.
Everything may feel uncertain, unpredictable,
and ever-changing in this world . . . BUT,
I'm here. You are a wonderful human being,
a fantastic mom, a perfect best friend, a
great sister, and a loving daughter. You are
loved. You are appreciated. You are special.
Obviously.

SOULMATE

Hey you, you're the most wonderful human being in the history of human beings. You've always given me the freedom to be myself and love me because of my crazy, not in spite of it. Yes, I have had love, but you will always be my soulmate. Besties for life. Lover you. Always, always. <ooo>

ANNIVERSARY LOVE

Lauren,

Our meeting was fate.

Becoming friends was our choice.

But falling in love with you was destiny.

Happy Anniversary, my Sweet!

Love,
MJ

ANNIVERSARY LOVE

Happy Anniversary, Mom and Dad.
70 years and still talking to each other!

With much love

I know I'll never be the perfect man for you. But I also know I'll never stop trying. I literally ache when I think of you and you're not there. I am in love with every single part of you, and that will never change.

Happy day of birth to the very best mama a little girl could ask for! I love you so much and it's so easy to see how much Elizabeth loves you when she stretches out those arms for "Ma Ma Ma Ma." Thank you for all you do for our girl.

Today is a good day because you are not just my sister, but my best friend.

I love you more than all the dogs in the world.

CONGRATS!

Sara Bell, HJ, and Stevie,

We are beyond stoked for you all. Get ready, get set, and enjoy the toughest yet most rewarding journey possible. And Stevie, please don't poop in the crib. Not cool.

Love,
Kel, JJ, and Roy

HAVE MUCH BELLY RUB AN GOOD WALKS

Hapi muders day to da bestest mommy ever. Yous deserves lots of pets an treats. To help celebrate Lilo promised no to chews on yous clotheses.

Ya and stich promised not to shed and be dumb!

Stichie not dumb mommy. Stichie love you mommie!

We all love you and hope you have much belly rub an good walks. But no baths.

Dear Mal, There is no way we could ever, ever thank you enough for donating a part of your body to my Mikal. He thought the road was ending, and lo and behold you offer your kidney to him, and all is changed. It was simply a miracle. You are a miracle! You deserve so much more than flowers, but we hope they express some small part of our gratitude for you, and for the life you helped extend.

With all our love,
Jean, Joe, and Steven

LOVE

Yeah, still thinking of you.

-Z

LOVE

Yep, you're still on my mind.

-Z

Welp, it's officially never changing. You're my girl, now and forever.

-Z

Nuni,

Today is your last day of school as a raspberry! We're so proud of you for finishing your raspberry year, so we got you flowers in your favorite color: rainbow!

Love,
Mommy, Daddy & Aya

ROMANCE

My queen! You, my love, made me a king. Our love is paradise and I will never live without you again. My heart is yours, now and forever.

Remember to go to the orchard and flower place soon. You always feel better planting and growing things. You are doing a great job. Smile. Each day on its own.

Papa, I am sending you 3 plants to represent 3 wishes I make for you on this day. May they teach you, as you teach us. May they help you breathe, as you've given us breath. And may they give comfort and companionship, as only my Daddio can. I love you!

LOVE

Flowers need the sun, even in the dew, everyone in this world knows that I love you. Years fly by, and tho they try, they can't stop me from loving you till the day that I die.

Babe, you continuously, neverendingly, always always make me laugh, turn me on, fire me up, and make my heart skip beats. I miss you and can't wait to see you later this week. This is our moment!

TE AMO

Tomorrow marks six months since meeting you, six months of laughs, love, and friendship. It's amazing how quickly the time has passed. I hope that the next six months are filled with joy and growth for both of us. I'm excited to continue getting to know you. I'm looking forward to all the kisses we will share, the adventures we will go on and the love that keeps on growing between us.

Te amo, siempre ♥

Chelsea,

I am a lucky dad to have a wonderful
daughter like you!! Happy Birthday and the best
to you forever!! I hope your day is fantastic
and I look forward to seeing you soon. Always
be careful and listen to your old Dad.

Love,
Daddy

LOVE

Every moment with you feels like magic. You came out of nowhere and stole my heart and soul but I love it because I feel safe, warm, and full—as a human being—with you. I love you.

Just a friendly reminder from you to you: Your booty is perfection. Your eyes are the light. You can smile and literally light up a room. Your mind is magnetic. You are way more than cool. You are always, always, always enough, and you're crushing this thing called life.

Love,
Yourself

Dear Roni,

A little sweetness for the best family we know. We know it isn't easy sending Seth off to college. Big hugs to all! It seems like yesterday when we met that cute 2-year-old, curly red-haired boy :)

Lots of love,
Liz and Mark

BIRTHDAY LOVE

Happy Birthday, Honey,

This bouq is called "Queen" and though we aren't royalty, your love and warmth rule my world. You continue to inspire me to be a better man for you and our three kids. I love you. More than you could know.

Spring is in the air! Or is that love? Can't remember—all I know is that you are in every breath of air I take.

Love you,
B

LOVE

For our love that is just as uncommon, I give to you Roselilies. Roselilies are born of a virus that causes the flower to grow more beautiful despite its flaws. Just like our love that started out as everyone thinking we were crazy and trying to keep us apart, and which has now bloomed into a romance beyond compare.

Nothing in life can hurt so bad that Grandma can't fix it. Thank you for mending my wounds, healing my soul, and filling my heart with all of your warmth, love, and goodness. I love you. Happy Grandparents Day!

FRIENDS

To my friend, across time and space

I hope these will put a smile on your face

Taylor,

A year ago we married each other!! I am fairly certain that was the second-best thing I have done in my life. The unquestionable first was falling in love with you.

I love that I get to take this short walk, called life, with you by my side. And I love you. I couldn't feel luckier.

Matt

Dearest Tina, Anyone can get you flowers, but only from me will you receive Volcano Roses from Ecuador because you engulf my heart in molten lava and set it on fire. I hope you remember that and also remember that true love has no monetary value attached to it. I ask only for your time, your company, your heart, and a place to rest my weary head when I visit because that's all I can give in return.

I love you very much . . . Charles

Dear Patti,

Just writing you this little note to say . . . YOU
DON'T NEED NO MAN TO SEND YO FLOWERS!

Love,
Me

E, the number 2 will forever hold a special place in my heart now. It's been 20 days since our amazing rooftop wedding in the sky, and the magical feeling just goes on and on. Let these flowers be an IOU for that tropical honeymoon that we'll eventually get to take. Fiji?

Love you forever and always,
S

P.S. LIMITLESS

Beauty helps protect the spirit of mankind, swaddle it and succor it, so that we might survive. You are beautiful! You are kind, courageous, and sincere. Keep on sharing from your deep well of wisdom, compassion, and charity. You help others to give and live more beautifully.

My heart sang solo, until it found you.

ROMANCE

Emilia,

When I see something gorgeous, I think only of
you, every time. Here and there, that something
is a garden of flowers—fresh, alive, vibrant
and pure—like you and the joy you spread daily.
I love you and will be with you soon.

Cheers to a lifetime together!

With love,
Ryan

Hi Mom,

Your birthday continues. You will receive flowers every month for the rest of the year. Hopefully these flowers will brighten your day and make you smile that beautiful smile.

We love you,
Pamela & David

My darling,

The name of this bouquet is "Que Sera Sera," which is also the song Doris Day performed in a Hitchcock film.

Here's to us . . . whatever will be, will be.

Love you always,
Chas

LOVE

Nothing can stop us. Let alone a little distance.
Love you.

ANNIVERSARY LOVE

Happy 40th Anniversary.

It seems like just yesterday . . . Not!

I continue to love and treasure you for the rest of our happy adventure together.

With lots of hugs and xxx's

Did you know that sunflowers reach toward one another when there is no sun? They turn to one another for support and energy when the light is darkest. Just like you and me. So, Sunflowers for you! You deserve it! Love you.

Sal, thanks for being the strength I've always needed and for showing me the way to just be me.

LOVE

To my sweetheart, I love you with all my soul.
Without you, I am nothing without you . . .
a butterless roll. I promise to love you for
years more, even when your bosoms sag down
to the floor.

ANNIVERSARY LOVE

18 years! 18 years and I've never loved you more than I do right at this moment. And it grows every day.

Love you, baby.

You the one!

Grampa, thank you so so much for carving the box to hold my special things. It means more to me than I can say.

AJ

SOULMATES

Friend >>>> Lover >>>> Boyfriend >>>>
Fiancé >>>> Husband >>>> Co-Parent >>>>>
Soulmate

LOVE

I'm not perfect, but together we are. I love us!

Lavender is for lovers. They mean enchantment, calm, and connection. This closeness is what defines us, my sweet, sweet love. This transcends you and me, and together we'll transcend all.

Lexzi,

Difficult roads often lead to beautiful destinations. Always remember how loved you are by all of us. And keep your head up, always. We can't wait to see you.

Jenny,

May this little mason jar of care bring some warmth and love and kindness right next to you in your day. I pray you feel warm all over, as though I am right there with you, sitting next to you, and just enjoying our shared space together. I love you and am always so glad you exist. You are so dear to me. Love you always.

BIRTHDAY LOVE

There's no way I could forget this day,
because there is no way I will ever forget
a woman as beautiful as you.

Happy Birthday,
Christine

Donna, my love,

Spring is a great time to be in love, but every season with you is so incredible!

I love you, Donna, and look forward to the rest of our lives together.

Loving you eternally,
Phil

ROMANCE

Gina,

How you feel right now..........

......That's how I feel,
Every time I see you.

B

"Ant" Sue,

Remember . . . you still look 30, and you're gorgeous, who else can really say that?

Love you so much!
Stacie

Thank you for being so good to me.

You are beautiful. You are intelligent.
You are special.

You have too many amazing qualities to list!!

LOVE

I wish I could turn back the clock. I'd find you sooner and love you longer.

You're a cunning, pliable, golden-haired sunfish, and nothing can stop you. Marriage? Done. Career? Pshh, nailed it. Master's degree while working full time? Give me something hard. Purchasing a home? Gonna nail that too, whether this house or another. Do it. Fierce. Power. You are the hardest-working and most inspiring human I have ever met or known, and every day I am proud to call you my friend.

Every day may not be good, but there's something good in every day. Work with the not so good, but celebrate the good! I'm here for it all: the good, the bad, the in-between. And I'm here for you.

Love,
Jenny

LOVE

This morning, I woke to the sunlight streaming through the window and I had an unstoppable feeling of joy. My heart knew at that moment that I love you. And that I will love you, always. Forgive my inability to express this feeling in this short note—I am no author, and never will be. But what I do know is that I love you and want to spend every waking (and sleeping) moment with you, till death do us part.

To my favorite parents,

For this milestone date, I hope you know
how much love and joy you have brought to
your children, grandchildren, extended families,
friends, and loved ones through your ongoing
partnership and union. Happy GOLDEN
anniversary! Congratulations!

P.S. I'm so glad I chose you.

A golden string no one can see has bound us from the start. Our very, very precious sister, it's love that ties our hearts.

Mom/Tay, You are an amazing woman, mother, and partner. What you have accomplished and managed over the past year would overwhelm almost anyone. You have handled everything that has come your way with grace. Take today (and this weekend) to treat yourself, soak in your amazing home, all the things you have accomplished, and the smile on your son's face. We are yours.

Love,
Zachary and Matthew

Sunflowers to remind you of me (they're my fav)
Thistles to remind you of the Highlands (home)
All of my love in a bouquet to show you that
you live in my heart and I'll always be here
for you.

I love you all with my whole heart!

Cass, I know life is dark and bleak right now, but know that there is always light. Whether it is the blooms of a tulip, or the hug from someone who cares, there are always reasons to smile even if it's along with some tears. I hope these can brighten your day just a little bit.

If you were the entire universe, it would be enough. You complete me.

To my dearest Valentine—

Give us a hundred lifetimes, and I would always find and choose you.

Happy Valentine's Day!

Love,
The man to whom you're related by marriage

My brother,

I love how you gave Gramma Daisy her flowers while she was living. Yes, you gave her those beautiful flowers every month so she could love and appreciate them. You also facilitated a space, as you do, for Gramma Daisy to continue what she loved, bringing joy to others. So she could share her flowers too. I love you, and want to love you in this way too.

I love you because:

You're okay with my crazy weekend ideas
Of your brain (not to eat, just to admire)
You make the bed with a keen precision
You hold my hand when we sleep
Because every thread of you is woven together
to make this incredible human.

PARA MI AMOR

Para mi amor,

I can't believe this will be our second Christmas together, life with you has been filled with happiness, growth and adventure. Thank you for being my lover, my best friend and partner in life.

Let's keep going!
I love you.

Hey, Mom!

I figured you could use a special little TGIF "just because I love you & you're the best mom ever" present. I saw these and it made me think of being at home in the desert with you and Choodles. I chose the one with 3 succulents, one for each of the Three Musketeers :) Love & miss you gals bunches!! I can't wait to see you in June and for our Hawaii reunion trip! :D

ROMANCE

To Tina,

A bouquet of angels for you . . . the one and only angel of my heart, whose wings take me high above the clouds and make even the birds envious in our flight.

Love always,
Charles

Grandmom,

To the woman who taught me what love really looked like: you've loved me every day of every week, you've loved me enough to ask the hard questions, you've loved me no matter how far I've strayed from home. I am so lucky to be surrounded by your love.

ANNIVERSARY LOVE

To Rafael and Sweets,

Here are 72 roses—one for every year together.
What an achievement and an inspiration.
Enjoy the day!

With love,
Jim and Kathy

Because you're much more beautiful than a dozen roses, here's two.

Love,
Hubby

Nancy,

You are Beautiful, Smart, Loved, Missed ever
so much! Wish we were there to clean the
house, cook for you, wash the clothes, and
most of all take care of you! You are the
Sunshine in our life. May these sunflowers bring
much joy to your room and think of us when
you look at them. We are praying for your
quick recovery and sending Angels your way.

Much love to you,
Gwen & Patrick OXOX

I know I have nothing to fear—even if the moon refused to rise and the stars stopped twinkling, I know I have my guardian angel watching over me and keeping me safe. I love you, Jacob, now and for eternity.

Aunt Georgia, You are always essential to me. Your love and care and kindness have always been a cherished haven for my heart and world. I love and miss you. I think of you and pray for you every single day. With these flowers, I pray some hope like springtime can fill your heart. Loving you always.

BIRTHDAY LOVE

You exist. You matter. You are enough. Full stop.
Happy Birthday, A. I have enjoyed experiencing
your journey. Here's to this brand-new journey
around the sun. So glad you are here.

My Dearest Love: You are my sunrise and sunset, and I long for the day to finally arrive when I won't miss either one without you. I love you very much, darling!

Love Always,
Charles

Lisa! I want to thank you for being a tremendous friend in general but particularly these past summer months. Thank you for phone calls, the text check-ins, the prayers & kind words in the mail. So honored to still be in your circle of care and to be connected to a woman who loves boldly and leads with integrity, compassion, and purpose. Sending love & gratitude to you!

Deep peace,
Marte

If I weren't an old, cranky septegenarian I would worship at your beautiful feet. I can't though—because I might not get back up. I hope it's the thought that counts.

SOULMATES

Kelly, I should have remembered your name.
I now know it, because it is imprinted in my
heart forever.

Because I love to make you smile . . . and because I'm not allowed to order you pizza.

2 Truths and a Lie . . . GO!

*I love you *I need you *I want you.

P.S. Trick question—all true!

Happy Birthday, my Bride!

NOTE TO SELF

You are capable of great things!

From,

me

TE QUIERO HERMOSA

Hi, amor,

Because you are you, and you're all I want this holiday season. I hope you feel the same joy in sharing moments with me; your laugh melts my heart, your kisses give goosebumps every single time . . . I'm obsessed with you & I am so excited for all that there is to come, this is just the beginning, baby.

Te quiero hermosa ♥

We might be worlds away, but you are close in our hearts & minds. 10 years is just the first leg of your journey. And all of your progress— has been together. You have built a fantastic life. As partners you take on your celebrations & obstacles as a team. And you love each other. There is so much to celebrate in that. Please know that we are celebrating (from afar) with you both today. We love you. Happy anniversary!

LOVE

You are the beacon of light and hope in my life, the beam that shoots through the fog and guides me home. With love, James

To my sweetest love on the sweetest of all days. My life just wouldn't be the same without you in it; in fact, it would be all the poorer and devoid of all of the joys you bring me on any given day just knowing that I am yours. I love you the world over, miss you ever so much, and long for the day when we will finally be together. Happy Valentine's Day, my darling!

Love,
Chas

Congratulations on the new journey!

We are rooting for you, with or without your smile, your big-girl panties, and your power pose! You've got this! Love, confidence, and power!

The WOMEN of the Accountability Group!

SOULMATES

True love is falling in love with the same person over and over again over time. Given our 20 years, I'd say we are "true."

BIRTHDAY LOVE

Happiest of B-days Michelle! You. Are. Amazing.
You are like a fine vintage of wine—every year
you get better (and I want to drink you up).

I love you,
Slope

NOTE TO SELF

INHALE THE FUTURE, EXHALE THE PAST.

TE AMO

Te amo.

Even a year later, and I know I will for
many more years, whether it be as a lover,
as a friend, or anything you want from me.
I know that there will always be love for
you in my heart.

Thank you for spending 365 days with me,
I cherished every single one.

Dearest Mom,

With this bright bunch we send all our love
and hopes that they'll bring cheer to your day
and this sad week. We thought they looked like
something Dad might have picked out for you
at the farmer's market, so it's fitting that
they arrive on his birthday—minus the roses, of
course—those are pure Jim! :)

We love you so much!
hugs and kisses

Dearest Tina,

Happy International Kissing Day, my darling!
Your kisses are definitely worth the wait!

I love you very much!!!

Forever yours,
Charles

You're amazing at what you do, always and forever. Don't let them take away any more of your glory. Please remember that your aura will always outshine their lackluster hearts. Keep pushing, because honey, you are destined for greatness. I told you years ago. Just keep believing, and put in that work . . .

For 5 years we've lived this life of magic and love together. 5 years of lasting memories. 5 years of daily gifts. No matter the ups or the downs, I see only the precious love I have for you. From 5 until forever!

LOVE

These blooms are my love for you—infinite and everlasting!

**LOVE (NOTES) BONUS!
A FREE BOUQS.COM GIFT CARD
JUST FOR YOU**

$10 Off

Enjoy $10 off farm-fresh flowers,
plants, and gifts on Bouqs.com.

Use code **BQNC1485PVXE4621**

One per customer, applicable on one item only, not combinable. Expires 12/31/23 at 11.59pm (PST).

**LOVE (NOTES) BONUS!
A FREE BOUQS.COM GIFT CARD
JUST FOR YOU**

$10 Off

Enjoy $10 off farm-fresh flowers,
plants, and gifts on Bouqs.com.

Use code **BQNC6357WBFL9574**

First published in the
United States of America in 2023 by
Universe Publishing, A Division of
Rizzoli International Publications, Inc.
300 Park Avenue South
New York, NY 10010
www.rizzoliusa.com

Author: John Tabis
Learn more at JohnTabis.com

Cover, p. 1: iStock.com/SvetlanaParsh
Publisher: Charles Miers
Associate Publisher: James Muschett
Editor: Elizabeth Smith
Design: Stislow Design
Production Manager: Colin Hough Trapp
Managing Editor: Lynn Scrabis

Printed in China

2023 2024 2025 2026 /
10 9 8 7 6 5 4 3 2 1

ISBN: 978-0-78934-142-6
Library of Congress Control Number:
2022940260

VISIT US ONLINE
Facebook.com/RizzoliNewYork
Twitter: @Rizzoli_Books
Instagram.com/RizzoliBooks
Pinterest.com/RizzoliBooks
Youtube.com/user/RizzoliNY
Issuu.com/Rizzoli